MISCHIEVOUS MOLLY DISCOVERS HER GIFT

Copyright © 2023 by MacKelly Books

All rights reserved

First edition, 2023

Illustrations and book cover by Lauren Zurcher
Book design by Spring Cedars

ISBN 978-1-950484-82-9 (paperback)
ISBN 978-1-950484-83-6 (hardback)
ISBN 978-1-950484-84-3 (ebook)

Published by Spring Cedars
Denver, Colorado
www.springcedars.com

Mischievous Molly Discovers Her Gift

written by
NANCY HALLOWELL and AFSOON KELLY

illustrated by
LAUREN ZURCHER

To Flannery, Miriam, Ramona and Virginia —

I hope our story inspires you to discover and share your gift fearlessly!

Nancy Hallowell
June 2024

SPRING CEDARS

My name is Molly. My parents call me Mischievous Molly. I am always getting into trouble.

I refuse to eat my vegetables.
No broccoli or carrots for me, please!

I do my best to wake up late and miss the school bus. No school for me, please!

This is Mojo. We found her at an animal rescue. She is my best friend on four legs.

Mojo and I play games, read books, watch stars, and fall asleep together.

Lucky for me, Mojo likes vegetables, especially when they come from my plate.

She also reminds me to close the front door and helps clean my mess.

And Mojo never gets mad when I miss the school bus. Like me, she loves riding in the car with Dad.

At school today, I have a new assignment.
"Write a story about your special gift," says Ms. Kim.

Is it someone's birthday?
Are we having a party? Do we get cake?

"A gift doesn't have to be wrapped in pretty paper and a shiny bow," our teacher explains. "It can be a special skill you share with others."

Hmmm, I don't know if I have a special gift. Mojo might have an idea.

Maybe my special gift is singing?
Mojo disagrees!

Maybe my special gift is painting?
Mojo disagrees!

Maybe my special gift is hitting a baseball? Mojo disagrees!

Frustrated, I stomp into the kitchen. "Mom! I must be good at something besides being mischievous!"

"You are a clever girl with a big heart," Mom says. "You will find your special gift. Why don't you visit your friend Ava? She is home with a bad headache."

I take Mojo with me to see Ava.

As Ava pets Mojo, she says, "It's been lonely at home. This is the happiest I have felt all day!"

"My Grandpa Joe says he also gets lonely at the retirement home," Ava says.

"Really?" I ask. "Maybe Mojo and I can cheer him up too!"

Grandpa Joe is very happy to see us. He gives Mojo a biscuit, and she gives his hand a big, wet kiss.

"Let's go down the hall to see my friend Mr. Pete," says Grandpa Joe. "I bet he would love to meet you and your sweet dog."

We visit Mr. Pete and a lot of other people. Everyone loves Mojo. This is fun! I like cheering people up.

"You brought the gift of joy to many lonely people today," Grandpa Joe says. "You two would make a great therapy dog team."

"What's a therapy dog team?" I ask.

"A therapy dog team has a kind person, like you, and a friendly dog, like Mojo. Together, you help people feel better by visiting them in places like retirement homes, hospitals, libraries, and schools."

Hmmm, I could go to school with Mojo? That sounds awesome. I race home to ask my parents for permission.

"Great idea!" Dad says. He arranges a meeting with Sara at Children's Hospital who will test us as a team.

I am nervous because I don't know what to do, but Mojo shows me the way.

As Sara watches, Mojo helps me meet other kids. We talk about their pets, school, all sorts of things.

The doctors and nurses are excited to meet us too. Seeing so many smiles makes me happy. I hope we can come here again.

"You and Mojo are a fantastic therapy dog team," Sara says. "This vest and tag will make it official."

My parents look proud, and so does Mojo.

"We did it, Mojo! We found my special gift! You and I are going to have so much fun helping others and spreading joy as a therapy dog team."

I can't wait to share my story with the class.

Everyone has a special gift.
What is yours?

_____

_____

_____

_____

Let us know and see what others say
by visiting us online, where you can also find
additional activities and resources.

www.MacKellyBooks.com

About the Authors

Nancy Hallowell retired from a 35-year career in marketing and public relations working in non-profit trade association, financial services, technology, and healthcare. Today, she is a youth tennis coach, helping kids discover and cultivate their best selves. Nancy has raised and trained service dogs. As an Alliance of Therapy Dogs member, she is a pet therapy volunteer at UC Health in Aurora, CO.

Afsoon Kelly graduated from CU Boulder in Economics and International Affairs and has worked in finance, technology, and operations in New York, Boston, and now Denver. She loves water sports, playing tennis, hiking, biking, and spending time with family and friends. In her ideal world, every child has a home, healthy food, and can express their talents regardless of race, ethnicity, or finances.

About the Illustrator

Lauren Zurcher is an award-winning children's book illustrator from Colorado. She began her journey as an artist when drawing about family vacations across the world. The geography, peoples, fauna, and culture are the source of her inspiration. Lauren lives in New York and loves bringing stories to life with colorful and playful visuals. For more, visit www.bylaurenzurcher.com.

Printed in the USA
CPSIA information can be obtained
at www.ICGtesting.com
JSRC081003121223
52974JS00010BA/132